A POET'S DIARY

The Mind of a Parkie

By

Stan Bryant

Printed in the United States of America

First Printing, December 2015

ISBN-13:
978-1519585974

ISBN-10:
1519585977

BabyGirlX Publishing

Edited by Emm Paul

Cover Design by Angie Zambrano

This book is dedicated to all those who suffer from Parkinson's, and just as important, to all the unselfish care givers who give their time and a big part of their life to assure the best care and quality of life possible under the circumstances

WE ONLY SEE THE OBVIOUS

As I peer across the valley,
my eyes glance upon a flock of sheep
some steadfast in their grazing
others fast asleep

I count perhaps a hundred
for their as far as the eyes could see
but one stands out among the rest
that's when it occurs to me

Among the flock of many
why is just one different from the rest
that's when I stop and realize
it's just the way my eyes digest

For not just one but all are unique
in their own special way
but we only see the obvious
the one that's clear as day

Like a trick of the mind we only conceive,
what we see without a thought
for not only one is different
but everyone in the flock

So next time you walk amongst the crowd
don't feel so out of place
for there are as many different people
as there are in the human race

WELCOME TO YOUR NEW WORLD

Welcome to the new world friend
no sense to bring your mind
you will find everything you need
just leave your thoughts behind

With just the push of buttons
all's at your finger tips
no need to try and think life through
the diodes and micro chips

I never have to worry
because I know I'm never wrong
my life is just so easy now
as long as my computer stays on

It thinks for me and plans my day
even tells me where to go
no sense in trying to remember things
it tells me what I know

I live through my computer
it's my friend and family
it takes me places around the world
places I would never see

But it also takes the joy and fun
of being there first hand
or to have a family sit and talk with a voice
instead of texting them by hand

A room full of people, yet not a sound
just fingers punching keys
what's become of family togetherness
what's become of me

GO AHEAD AND CRY

If you feel no matter what you do
and despite how hard you try
things just seem to fall apart
then go ahead and cry

If you feel you're on a one way street
and the directions the wrong way
and you're not gaining any ground
go ahead cry, but just don't stay

When you feel you're in this world alone
and all hope for you is gone
cry and let the pain be known
but cry and then move on

When you're body starts its path
and it fights every move you make
just keep fighting, never give in
cry then give it all you can take

When the night comes and goes
and you haven't slept a day or two
keep on going , it will come
and cry when the pain is through

Never be ashamed to let it out
or to tell anybody why
and soon you will find it in your heart
to laugh and cry, cry, cry

THE POET AND THE PRINCESS

For I am just a man of words
a poet some might say
I only put on paper, things
to give you hope throughout the day
my words might have but little sense
or perhaps, what you seek to find
I only tell what lays deep in my soul
or perhaps what's in my mind
but I to seek the comfort of things
that makes me laugh just because
I want to feel the taste of joy, the smiles
the dreams of unfiltered life that was
I want to act that of a silly child
running wild across the fields and hills
to pretend of times we sat for tea
and sipped wine , how real it feels
For being a child, though all grown up
we still have dreams that can come true
a man of words and a princess
I the poet, the princess, you
for I did not feel I'm worthy of a friend
with such beauty and such grace
for many times I have glanced
your beauty, but I felt so out of place
but the princess and the poet
she smiles with all her grace
I do as well just knowing
that she enjoys my company
and the toast of wine glasses
the coffee and the tea

A CAREGIVER IS A GIFT FROM ABOVE

I carry this disease by no choice of my own
carry it with me through body and bone
a caregiver has the choice to leave or to stay
to take on the burdens I face every day
My quality of life that I live from here in her hands
giving up part of hers I'm sure wasn't her plans
but she takes all the bickering, my ups and my downs
she takes my bad days, and turns them around
at times when I shake like a bird in the cold
she comforts my soul and offers her hand to hold
not a word is said, when I drop things time over again
she follows behind , cleaning up where I've been
like clockwork, every four hours it's medicine time
she often forgets hers, but never mine
she knows more about me and what to expect
she's read about everything , then double checked
if you want to learn from those who seen it first hand
ask a caretaker, they understand
if someone chooses to stay out of caring and love
I would believe they're a gift from above

I'M SORRY IF I TOOK IT OUT ON YOU

I'm sorry if I took my anger
and poured it out on you
its only because you do for me
the things I used to do
I never mean to hurt you
by the things that I might say
I'm only angered at myself
not you in any way
it's hard when I can't be
the man that I use to be
instead of helping you now
it is you who's helping me
I lost the strength I use to have
my pride has been knocked down
and I have no one else to tell
so I vent when you're around
I don't take time to stop and think
how much you really care
and I don't realize how much you mean
until you are no longer there
it's by far not your fault
nor is it any thing you do
it's only because you're there
that I take it out on you
I say how much I wish
that you had never come along
and how much better off I'd be
if only you were gone
these words of hurt and anger
that would tear others apart
yet you never leave my side because
you know they're not coming from my heart
when I'm feeling down
you know I best like to be alone

you are always somewhere close to me
but leave me on my own
in a very understanding way
you carry me through life
I would never want you to feel any way
but loved, my wonderful, loving wife

THE WONDERS OF HEAVEN

As I stare into the vastness
of a moon lit night
there's a multitude of beauty
in each twinkling of a light
each has its own wonder
each answer left to find
only seen , but vaguely
by the imagination of the mind
how far must you go
till you can see the end
and once you are there
does it start all over again
is there really places
that is comforting as here
if so how far away
or better yet how near
would we be just as we are
if the world was in a different place
or would we be just as ignorant
no matter where in space
just a grain of sand
on a never ending beach
so much we need to learn
yet no one there to teach
perhaps outside our world
was meant only to be seen
but left un touched by human hands
and viewed but in our dream
so many questions ,left to ask
the answer might be clear
why look at other worlds
when you see what we did here
everything was created
with perfection of god's hand
but it didn't suit us

so it was changed by man
you think if we were somewhere else
we would change the things we could
and if so would it be, for worse
or for our own good
we were given nature
to support the human race
if you can find an untouched land
you'll find a perfect place

CAN'T PLANT SEEDS ON CONCRETE AND STONE

I sit down beside a rigid ole man
a pipe in his mouth, newspaper in hand
I could see by the look in his eyes
he's a man of few words, but one that is wise

He said can't plant fields this time of year
with the snow and the wind, won't last I hear

He said he's been a farmer most all of his life
raising the crops just him and his wife

But you can't plant seeds on concrete and stone
that's all that's left of the land that I owned

They took our land where we plowed and we tilled
put up the malls where once was our field

This bench here where I sit every day
once was our home where we use to pray

But still I come every day, like clockwork it seems
to walk on the ground that once held our dreams

As I stood I reached to shake his hand and say our
goodbyes
I noticed his limp and the tears in his eyes

As I walked away, I noticed a stone near the walk
it read "Here she lays with a heart like a rock".

THE CITIES OF OLD

In the cities of old, lay treasures untold
many die for the sake of its wealth
promises of riches, they dig and leave ditches
all taking toll on their health

They put scars through the land, to get gold in their
hand
yet tear down a mountain for such
or trees they cut down and alter the ground
destroying the land that they touch

For it is bare no nature left there
where once was a beautiful place
now just dirt lines the path where once was grass
nothing left but open space

Tear down a mountain or more for a pocket of ore
the reason doesn't make sense
or a hillside of trees for the nice luxuries
and then more for an unneeded fence

To keep out or keep in, nothing left to defend
so miles of fence there's no need
to see such a waste, all done in haste
and all done by the human breed

I'm not proud of our race, or the destruction we face
just for the greed of our kind
we take nature and grace, and make wasteland in place
soon there shall be none to find

FOLLOWED A PATH TO THE HIGHEST HILL

As I follow the trail to the highest ridge
I glance at the valley below
I ponder and stop it crosses my mind
as I watch the streams that flow

How many have stood in my steps
and seen such beauty as I
and was given the grace to see what I see
above where only eagles fly

The carpet of colors that grace the land
the snow capped peaks of white
such beauty of nature a gift from god
each view is pure delight

Traces of life, yet so long before
remnants of a cabin nature reclaims
where once burnt the warmth of a fire
a chimney of only stones remain

I still hear the echo of the children playing
as the hunters set out for their winters meat
the smell of the smoke as the chill sets in
the rustling of twigs from the hunters feet

Again I look and realize
it was but a vision in my own mind
yet another gift, a chance to see
what beauty, if you look you may find

OUTSIDE MY WINDOW

There's a whole new world outside my window
though I've seen it every day
I chose to take a closer look
I see it a different way

I see the expressions on the face of a child
not just a passerby
I feel the ache of a rigid ole man
and stop to wonder why

I've only seen life from what my eyes perceive
my mind tells me there's more
the things that was there in front of me
that I failed to see before

But along with pain deep down inside
there's beauty there as well
if by chance you never look
you'll pass it by and not even tell

Everything outside my window
has more than what I see
look at things closer and you will find
what is there might not be

The eyes may fool the mind
but the mind can't fool the heart
so when you choose to look again
that's the place to start

HOW FAR TO THE END OF HEAVEN

How far to the end of heaven
where might it begin
does it go on forever
or is it a circle with no end
is there a place out there that's somewhere
yet nowhere at all
if you reach the end, is that the beginning
or perhaps there's just a wall
a place where old stars gather
for their time to shine is done
or do they join to form from millions of others
and combine into one
each set in a perfect place
and yet nothing to hold it there
and come the evening sunset
like clockwork you still see its glare
like life and its many wonders
who are we, why are we here, we ask
why are we so alike, yet so different
as well as our task
there must be a sun to keep us
from the darkness and the cold
there must be new stars born
to replace those of old
I believe each has his purpose
in this circle of life not by chance you see
everyone has a special purpose
here for this world to be
nor do I believe we were meant to be alone
for new life, everything takes two
life was never meant to live it alone
Together is how life grew

DEEP IN THE VALLEY

Deep in the valley
where it's cold and grey
lies the remnants of a temple
where they used to pray

Still standing upright
as if to welcome as before
remains the arched entry way
and a cross upon the door

Fog rolls across the valley
if you listen you can hear
the clamoring of footsteps
they sound so far and yet so near

The faint sound of chapel bells
and singing from its walls,
the silent sound of preaching words
from which our father calls

The temple dead with nature
yet so alive with past gone by
the silent sounds of those still praying
and the widows cry

As I leave this valley
though most the temple may not survive
the thought of those who once came to pray
their spirit keeps it alive

FEEL SORRY FOR MYSELF

Feel sorry for myself
for feeling sorry for me
I feel sorry for holding on to things
I should have long set free

I should have never wanted things
I really didn't need
I should have been happy with what I have
no more to show my greed

I feel the pain and hurt
just like any other man
yet I forget the times of joy
life that defined who I am

I had my share of laughter
I've felt love for all its worth
I've seen life taken but
I've also witnessed birth

The two sides to everything in life
the choice is yours to make
if you don't feel satisfied on the road you're on
choose a different one to take

THE WORLD'S A PERFECT PLACE

They say the worlds not a perfect place
to this I don't agree
look into natures wilderness
and tell me what you see
everything is perfect
each beauty has its place
only by the hand of man
Does this get erased
creation of every sort you see
each has purpose to this earth
for each that falls, another rises
it's the beauty of natures birth
everything man needs in life
in abundance can be found
enough for every living soul

Enough to go around
no need to see a child in hunger
or a man who has no home
or to see one person have enough
for fifty men alone
the world is a perfect place
it's the diversity and greed of man
that turns this perfect world around
and destroys it with his hand
the world was meant a place to live
to thrive and live as one,
but the greed of man destroys this land
soon we shall have none

LET HER GO AND WATCH HER FLY

Losing you is hard to do
though sorrows less as time goes by
all the things that we've been through
even angels have to cry

I feel the sadness and the pain
you cross my mind most every day
my tears flow down like summer rain
i shall go on come what may

The stillness fills the darkest night
an empty place inside my soul
they say that soon I'll see the light
but till then I won't be whole

The time has come to take her home
the choir sings, the church bells ring
she's no longer all alone
they came to take her in the spring

It was her favorite time of year
the flowers bloom, the frost is gone
the sounds of blue birds fill the air
as they sing her favorite song

They come to carry her away
the hardest parts, the last goodbye
she will spread her wings today
let her go, and let her fly

SHES EARNED HER WINGS TODAY

He's come to take his child home
up to where the angels pray
she is no longer all alone
she earned her angel wings today

No more tears shall ever fall
no more sadness, no more pain
today the angels came to call
to carry her home again

She carries with her no regret
each day she knelt beside her bed
she knows he will not forget
she'll be were angels only tread

A smile she will have for ever more
she's gods child once again
she's done gods given chore
she is forgiven of any sin

MY SCRIPT IN LIFE

I couldn't say if there's a role that's been cast
to dictate all the things that I've lived in my past
I only think, perhaps someday I will know
is there a higher power that's running the show

Is all the rights and wrongs written down in a book
when my play is over will I chance to look
or do we live life just one day at a time
and go in to tomorrow totally blind

Where every decision we make is that of our own
and there is no book that can ever be shown
for each mistake there's a price we must pay
the cost to repair it, the loss of a day

But what if every day we lived, was very well rehearsed
and all the mistakes we make could always be reversed
we could just keep living life over till we finally get it
straight
we wouldn't have to wonder because we'll already know
our fate

If you really think about it, is that the life you would
choose
even though you would know of everything and not a
thing to lose
is that a life worth living, no chances, no dreams, to fill
your mind
no mysteries or matinee, or secret places will you ever
find

No maternity rooms with pink and blue they know the
gender long ago
good or bad, I like each day to be one of a journey I
don't know

I choose not to live by a book, a script to define who I shall be
I want to write my own part in life, the one where I play me

ICE ANGEL

She's the devils own angel
she'll cast you a spell
she will take you to heaven
then drag you to hell

With wings of an angel
she's there to entice
the looks of a goddess
yet a heart made of ice

She walks through the forest
till someone comes in
as their lust over takes him
they never come out again

Enticed by her beauty
and sensual desire
the ice angel drags you
to the heart of the fire

HER PRINCE IS BUT A SIMPLE MAN

As the clock upon the wall strikes midnight
there's no pumpkins carriages nor queens
her prince is only but a simple man
in cowboy boots and jeans

For her love there is no fairytale
but yet a dream come true
her feet won't fit a ruby slipper
but her sandals will always do

Her horse drawn carriage has a bed
and a trailer pulled behind
their castle is a mobile home
but to them it is just fine

You need no ruby slippers
to feel as if a queen
nor no golden chariots waiting
to fill a woman's dream

The riches come from deep inside
for you a heart of gold
for love is that of great rewards
the greatest story never told

PARKINSON'S, WHO AM I?

I am the shaking with uneffortless will of my own
I am the pain in every muscle and bone
I am the twitching of your neck and your eyes
I am the false smile you wear as a disguise
I am the voice that no one can hear
I am the worries the hurt ,and the fear
I am the feeling of being alone and afraid
I am not one of the choices you made
I am the one who makes you feel out of place
I am the one who took the dreams that you chase
I am the one that keeps you up through the night
I am the one who makes life tougher to fight
I am the one who took your balance as well
I am the one who made your life living hell
I am the one who gave you strength to go on
I am the one who will make you ever so strong
I am what you choose to make of me
I am only as strong as you allow me to be

THE HURT IN YOUR EYES

You ever look into someone's eyes so close
you see their hurt and pain
it's a feeling that comes from deep down inside
one you can't explain

No matter how they try to mask it
the fact it's that it still shows
to some it stands out clear as day
to others they'll never know

The hurt stands out as if to cry
even in pictures it can't hide
the years of pain and misery
that's built up deep inside

Sometimes all it takes is just a few words
to show someone you care
if you want someone to listen
my dear friend I will be there

THE HARDER YOU PUSH I WILL PULL

There's a hurt that grows deeper than pain
with a few words I'll try to explain
when the things that you do, are things I used to
it constantly gnaws at my brain

If you tell me I can't, then I'll try
with no rhyme or reason why
I'll go along just to prove I'm still strong
even if it hurts till I cry

Don't tell me I won't then I will
regardless of how I might feel
I'll prove that I can, just to prove I'm a man
without making it a big deal

how far can I go till I'm done
I'll keep going till I feel I've won
perhaps even more, just to make sure
and say it was all done in fun

The harder you push I will pull
my glass is not half empty, its full
and till it is gone, I'll keep moving along
then when you say I gave up that is bull

If I happen to throw a small fit
it's only because I never quit
I might stop and rest, but I try my best
slower perhaps just a bit

But I'm still running this race
so what if I don't get first place
as long at the end I'm standing, my friend
I finish with love and grace

THE STEM AND THE ROSE

We see the beauty of the rose
but forget the thorny stem
we awe at the brilliant colors
but forget the strength within

Each rose handpicked and cut
and sorted with tender care
the strength beneath its beauty
lays hidden as if not there

All along its been the support
that held the rose up high
so each can gaze upon its glory
but the stem just gets passed by

There are times i am the stem
I give strength to all in need
other times I am the rose
my colors shine bright indeed

It's not important which I am
it takes both to grow
each as needed as the other
to let its beauty show

MY BEAUTIFUL ROSE OF PINK

Among my bright red roses
stands a pink rose all alone
the ground for which it grows upon
same dirt for which the others sewn

Care and love for each the same
yet its color of brilliant pink
it makes you stop and wonder why
it brings my mind to think

By chances it a reminder to us
that not everything in life is the same
and those that stand out among the crowd
should be cherished, not cast upon blame

I ponder at my rose of pink
I talk of it with honor and great pride
for it stands out as a proof of strength
it doesn't droop nor need to hide

It stands out among the rest of them
to see yes, it makes you stop and think
why can't we honor everything such as this
my wonderful rose of pink

TARNISHED RING OF BRASS

Among her box of priceless jewels
sits a ring of tarnished brass
no diamonds emeralds or priceless stones
but only a piece of glass

Yet all the riches the others hold
will never quite compare
to the bent and unpolished ring of brass
that she gives so little care

But though its worth is but just a dime
to her its priceless in her mind
given her though long ago
a memory of a love left long behind

A high school sweetheart, her only love
had placed it in her hand
and promised to return someday soon
and replace it with a wedding band

But duty called him to a faraway place
where he rests this very day
yet she still holds hope he will return
each night as she kneels to pray

She holds it on a necklace
as close to her heart as it could be
the tarnished ring of brass she holds
as she forever waits for me

TOGETHER WE CAN

How can we climb the mountain
if both of us are weak
if we climb it both together
we can climb its highest peak

Alone we stand no chance
to ever reach the top
but together there is nothing
that can ever make us stop

Put our minds together
we can do most anything
and conquer any obstacles
or challenges life might bring

Far too stubborn-headed
I've always tried it on my own
and stood waiting at the bottom
as others left me there alone

The challenges that face me
are not impossible to overcome
but it makes the climb much easier
when there's two heads not just one

AN ANGEL WEEPS

Beyond the clouds an angel weeps
her tears pour down like rain
her halo battered, her wings all torn
her heart again full of pain

For her own love she must carry home
and listen as the trumpets play
and carry him beyond the clouds
for this his final day

She weeps for the life they once shared
for the ones who are left behind
for those who stand and cry at his empty shell
not knowing they will meet again in time

For the journey god has given him
he has fulfilled every task
he has done more than his share in life
of him what more can you ask

Everyone will be called home some day
it should be a day of rejoice not sorrow
for you have met every challenge given you
whether it be today or perhaps tomorrow

When I retire from my life I live
and the day that my chores are through
I shall sit high above the clouds as well
and look down and weep for you

CARRY ME HOME IN THE ARMS OF AN ANGEL

Carry me home in the arms of an angel
when my time here is at its end
till then, just dust your wings off
I'll seek comfort from you now and then

For I know your wings are withered
trying to keep my soul in line
and the many times I've lost my way
you kept my heart from crying

My road was long and winding
I put new foot prints along its path
each foot step that I would take
I felt I took two steps back

If you shall come to call me
I'll come running arms open wide
but till that time I have living to do
so rest your wings upon your side

Then carry me home in the arms of an angel
when my journey's at its end
I then can say my life has been complete
and say goodbye my angel, my friend

THERE'S NOT ALWAYS A PAVED ROAD TO HEAVEN

There's not always a paved road to heaven
some times its of gravel and stone,
the one you take, depends on your choices
which one to lead you back home

I try to show every day that I'm grateful
for each new day He grants me
I don't try and take it for granted
that another day for tomorrow, a guarantee

Life at times may not seem to have a reason
the struggles and the hardships, unfair
but if it was all joyous times and sunshine
you would never appreciate what's there

If my choices lead me down gravel and stone
so be it, that's my chosen path
perhaps I will be granted the smooth road back
and spared from the treacherous wrath

I know I am not alone and the path is well lit
and He will always be alongside me
He will never lead me astray
because I am where He wants me to be

ALONE IN A ROOM FULL OF PEOPLE

Being alone with a heart full of pain
in a room full of people yet they refrain
perhaps their afraid to listen and learn
for it is but one thing, understanding I yearn

For I don't ask for their money, just time
yet that is too precious to waste on a soul such as mine
wont you just listen without turning away
or is it deaf ears, you don't care what I say

To be all alone is a pain hard to bear
but worst in a room full of people, yet no one to care
we don't choose what is given us through life's one way
ride
most go it alone because other's foolish pride

They carry the hurt and the pain all alone
they fear others see you as weak, your strength hasn't
shown
just to seek comfort from those that you trust
isn't an option, it is a must

Many will turn, this is no place for them
but keep going forward, there's no giving in
and amongst the sands soon a stone you shall find
and to those who don't listen, you must leave them
behind

My life's not about waiting for them to choose me
my life's about making it the way I want it to be

WOKE UP WONDERING WHO I REALLY AM

I woke up this morning wondering
who I really am
I go back and search my life
to when it all began,
I'm the child my mother loved
and held me in her arms
I'm the one my father raised
and kept me from harm

I'm the one who took my books
and gained the ways to live
I'm the one to understand
why not to receive but give
I've learned each day the choices
and which were right or wrong
and a man needs not wealth and fame
to be considered strong

I learned through life that mistakes are made
but I learned from them
I learned its only foolish
if you try the same mistake again
I've done my life's work and what I did
in my life I'm proud
inside my soul I'm happy with what I have
I don't need a roaring crowd

each day I wake and think to myself
how lucky that I am still me
I don't need the big things, or to run a race through
life I'm where I want to be
every days not perfect
but I have been given every day
and the chance to live it how I chose
and to live it my own way

What I've done in days that past
are days I've already lived
now I shall live each new day in life
there's a limit what he will give
this minute is the first of your future
make it the last one of your past
start today looking forward to times ahead
they don't forever last

FOLLOWED A PATH TO THE HIGHEST HILL

As I follow the trail to the highest ridge
I glance at the valley below
I ponder and stop it crosses my mind
as I watch the streams that flow

How many have stood in my steps
and seen such beauty as I
and was given the grace to see what I see
above where only eagles fly

The carpet of colors that grace the land
the snow capped peaks of white
such beauty of nature a gift from god
each view is pure delight

Traces of life yet so long before
remnants of a cabin nature reclaims
where once burnt the warmth of a fire
a chimney of only stones remain

I still hear the echo of the children playing
as the hunters set out for their winter's meat
the smell of the smoke as the chill sets in
the rustling of twigs from the hunter's feet

Again I look and realize
it was but a vision in my own mind
yet another gift, a chance to see
what beauty if you look you may find

I AM JUST A CLOWN

For you are that of a beautiful princess
I am but a circus clown
you have but a mighty kingdom
I move from town to town

Your flowing hair, your skin like silk
me with a painted on face
me with the grime and the dirt on my knees
you not a strand of hair out of place

For I am just a man of laughter and jokes
while you that of beauty and charm
what a foolish thought to even believe
of a princess with a clown at her arm

Although I'm just a clown on the outside
I am just as good a man as any deep inside
what could be the harm shall I go and meet the princess
at least I'll walk away and say I tried

As I approach there must have been a hundred guards
or more
but she raised her hand and they all knelt down
she reached her arm out to mine
she said everybody loves a clown

At least now there's laughter in the kingdom
and I cheer her up every time she's feeling down
not quite what I had in mind
but hey, everybody loves a clown

FRIEND FROM AFAR

To my dear friend MAR DIAZ

She sets upon her horse
as if a queen upon her throne
her beauty captures all who glance
perhaps a million eyes alone

A garden full of roses
in a vase of solid gold
is not enough to match her grace
that god on her bestowed

Just one glance as she rides away
her image still in mind
for you may search the world over
yet one such as her you'll never find

The distant waters though worlds away
I see her in my dreams
I cross the waters to her distant home
every night it seems

I know that I shall never kiss her lips
or hold her close to me
but I am graced to know her as a friend
a friend across the sea

DEVIL'S DAUGHTER

Thunder rolls across the sky
like the sound of a thousand stampeding horses
listen close you can hear their cry
her lustful eyes capture the riders' forces

Bolts of fire fly from an angered sword
she has come to seek revenge upon her mate
death to those can be assured
there's no escaping their fiery fate

A kiss of death with a tongue of lightning
just one strike you'll feel her wrath
her temptress ways are so inviting
she will take your soul if you cross her path

If you hear her pipers' playing
you will know they're on their way
if you don't you best start praying
she let you live another day

LOVE WITH JUST A PEN AND PAD

A flame needs but a single spark
to ignite the desire in ones soul
if only in imagination
the writings make it whole

They can take you any place
that you choose to be
they can dominate your mind
in total ecstasy

Can fill your wildest dreams
with but a stroke of pad and pen
I can make you a princess of love
or give you pleasure as if a sin

For I can make sweet love to you
with just the words I say
or I can fill my own desires
and simply walk away

Perhaps we'll make love through the night
until I fill your need
or simply seek our pleasure zone
until I hear you plead

PERFECT 10

One with such her beauty
for there is no one to compare
from her sultry eyes her silky skin
her flowing auburn hair

A princess is a simple word
it doesn't match her grace
a queen of queens, perhaps comes close
she's got everything in place

The image of a perfect girl
unspoiled by her charm
as she walks you expect to see
a king upon her arm

Yet alone in travels, untarnished
from what god has bestowed to her
I would give to her a perfect 10
or a perfect hundred if there ever were

SONG FROM ALL THE NOTES I SENT TO YOU

I'm going to write myself a love song
from all the notes I sent to you
then i make a million copies
send one as each day is through

Shall a million days go past me
and you're not back here where you belong
then I guess my words were useless
in my loving leaving song

I can't forget the day you left me
roses strewn across the floor
the smell of your perfume
and a note taped to the door

You said the man that I become
is not the man I use to be
and you no longer can pretend
you're no longer in love with me

If a million days of love notes
I'll send to you one each day
then I guess it's really over
and I should be on my way

And if you ever hear the drummer
play the drums to my love song
that's just the lonely beating of my heart
so go ahead and sing along

FOLLOWED A PATH TO THE HIGHEST HILL

As I follow the trail to the highest ridge
I glance at the valley below
I ponder and stop it crosses my mind
as I watch the streams that flow

How many have stood in my steps
and seen such beauty as I
and was given the grace to see what I see
above where only eagles fly

The carpet of colors that grace the land
the snow capped peaks of white
such beauty of nature a gift from god
each view is pure delight

Traces of life yet so long before
remnants of a cabin nature reclaims
where once burnt the warmth of a fire
a chimney of only stones remain

I still hear the echo of the children playing
as the hunters set out for their winters meat
the smell of the smoke as the chill sets in,
the rustling of twigs from the hunters feet,

Again I look and realize
it was but a vision in my own mind
yet another gift a chance to see
what beauty if you look you may find

The music played on

The dance went on from dusk till dawn
not a step was ever missed
when the lights went low they stole the show
and each bow he stole a kiss

They twirled and slid like the youth of a kid
as the band continued to play
as the music went on they danced every song
they would swirl bow and sway

For the first time in years, they heard the loud cheers
every one's eyes were on them
at the last curtain call, they bowed to them all
and rejoiced to their youth once again

They recalled younger years it brought them to tears
as the memories started to fade
but oh what a show, their face all aglow
the day that the music played

OCEAN OF TEARS

I walk the shores where we use to play
but that was yesterday and now you're gone
no words are spoken as I kneel and pray
since you went away, it seems so long

The sands of time can't erase the pain
once again I call to you
but nobody's listening, tears hid by rain
I cry an ocean they haven't a clue

Waves come in and wash away the sand
I hold in my hand, but just gets swept away
maybe to a far off land
maybe to a sunny place where the skies aren't so grey

I hear the sounds, of ships just off the coast
the echo of the sailors coming home
but the one that I long for most
is out there somewhere all alone

I place a rose on the shores of his watery grave
each day as the tide rolls in
the only sailor that they couldn't save
the sea had taken by the stormy wind

I walk the shores where we use to play
but that was yesterday, and now you are gone
no words are spoken, as I kneel and pray
since you went away, it seems so long

IF I COULD WRITE YOU IN MY WORLD

I could write you in my world
of dreams and fantasies
but that don't bring you any closer
to my world, of you here with me

And if I kiss you, only ink stains
on the lips I long to feel
as a constant reminder
that my dreams of you aren't real

Just broken pieces of my heart
lay shattered on the floor
once again I'm left to mend it
as I have, time and time before

The tear stains on my pillow
won't wash away the pain
of the times i felt the sorrow
they flow down like rain

The pen can change you and make you
whatever you wish to be
but even writings
can never bring you here to me

ALL HEARTS HEAL WITH TIME

If the extra weight upon your shoulders
seems more than you can bear
set me down, I'll walk beside you
till we can make it there

No need to pull you down with me
as just another victim of this pain
if you choose to walk away
there is no need to explain

The outcome of my future
though not written in any stone
remains the way I look at life
regardless, the choice is mine alone

I still have the strength to fight
until the bitter end
whether by myself alone
or with you my dearest friend

I ask nor have the right to
put your life away for mine
so go my dearest love
all hearts heal with time

ONE LESS LONELY HOUR

If you held me in your arms
for just an hour every day
that's one less lonely hour
I'll spend feeling this way

And if you tell me that you love me
though I know that's not quite true
I'll just go on pretending it is
and believe I'm still in love with you

And when we say good night
and turn in bed to face the other way
do you think of leaving me
or do you really wish to stay

When the sun shines through the window
and the bluebirds sing their song
is there a chance I'll turn one day
to find that you have gone

Two hearts that beat as one
is the love that we once shared
nothing could ever tear us apart
nothing ever even dared

But I'm no longer the same man
you married years ago
so I'm giving you the choice my dear
to love me or to go

GLASS HEART

No place to end
no place to start
I'm looking at love
through a glass heart

I peer at that which
to touch is so near
but the chance shall it shatter
is that which I fear

Then the crystal lay aground
like swords thrust at me
I leave it untouched
shall I just leave it be

Yet I yearn for her love
that's encased in the glass
the temptations to powerful
to just let it pass

Do I have what she needs
to break her wall in
I have but one chance
will I lose, will I win

I MUMBLE WHEN I TALK

Though you might not understand me
because I mumble when I talk
and though I'm slow at getting there
because I shuffle when I walk

I'd be glad to shake your hand
no effort needed there
I just want you to love for who I am
and take the time to care

I don't ask for sympathy
just a nice hello will do
or a simple smile now and then
to acknowledge I am there with you

My shaking's not contagious
or my shuffling of the feet
and if you need I'll write it down
though it won't be nice and neat

But there are things I must do differently
but the end results the same as you
yes it takes a bit more time
but I still manage to get through

I AM AN OCEAN

I am an ocean
my currents are strong
I can wake you or shake you
I could pull you along
for the wind strikes you're sails
all tattered and torn
I grasp you in my clutch
too far off shore to mourn
you may try and swim against me
many have tried
only to be lost
washed washed away with the tide
shall you wait till i settle
and the moon loses its grip
perhaps in my calmness
you shall finish your trip
let this be a lesson to heed
if you have any doubt
when the tides come swiftly in
don't try to swim out

GARDEN OF MARBLE
TO THOSE WHO GAVE IT ALL

As I look across the garden
of marbled stone
each is etched a name
of which many never made it home
I glance upon the hill top
to which there stands but one alone
and upon its marbled face it reads
here lies the tomb of the unknown
only to god do we know
who rests upon this sacred ground
it's a tomb for those lost in battle
for those never found
each stone another marker
of a hero who gave his all
each gave his life for freedom
for each the angels call
when I kneel beside my bed tonight
I wont pray for me alone
I give my prayers to those heroes
and god safely guide them home
when I complain I think of all my choices
my comforts of feeling free
then I stop to realize
they gave it all for me

THE QUESTION HURTS

When the grand kids ask how long it lasts
and why does grandpa twist and shake
will he ever get better like he use to be
how long does Parkinson's take

The question hurts much more than the answer
coming from the mind of a child
what do you tell them to ease their minds
and keep it from running wild

Will I be alright, of course they ask
with that sorrowed look in their eye
how did you catch it will it go away
every question is but another why

I can be as good as I want to be
I am still your same grandpa
I have it, it doesn't have me
that's when they give you that look of awe

It takes awhile to be ok
lots of adjustments then you go on
but I'm still your friend, your fishing buddy
and I shall be all along

So yes I'll be better, with encouragement from you
that will give me the strength I need
you are my inspiration to never give in
you are the reason I shall succeed

WOULD SAVE IT FOR MY WIFE

If I was given but one more hour
for each day I face this fight
as I quietly put away the time
and wipe her tears each night

And back the clock each day's end
each evening as I kiss her cheek
and before she starts her day
I would think about the time I keep

And soon an hour adds to a day
a day soon turns into four
and pretty soon perhaps a year
god knows I owe her more

And when my times is due here
if i should have any left at all
please give it to my loving wife
when my piper comes to call

Don't let me be the last one
that she will ever love
please hand to her the time I saved
when you take me up above

For her love and kindness in her heart
I've stretched it to the end
so give her now the time I've saved
so she may love once again

WHO SHALL I BECOME TODAY

Who shall I become today
a charming prince, a child at play
or perhaps I'll be a circus clown
next time they come to town

Or maybe an explorer of cities
long lost to through the years
or a bull fighter, a matador
the crowd roaring with cheers
.
Or maybe a astronaut
on a journey through space
I'll be the first one to step on
an uncharted place

There are many of things
I could wish I would be
but the best one of all
I just want to be me

A WONDEROUS TASK

Life could be a wondrous task
do we know how long it lasts
is there a time set in our mind
is there an answer for us to find

Do we go and jus simply fade away
or go beyond to where we pray
do welcome back and live again
do we return to where we've been

Do we live it with all its glory
yet have no ending to our story
there are two things ,you live and die
shall we ever know the reason why

What comes next when the two are done
is there more lives or only one.
to many questions with answers unknown
curious mind won't leave it alone

Too many spend their whole life worried about death
and do so till their final breath
life is for living each moment, each day
let god choose when He'll take it away

Don't put off living, no matter the case
for you're assured that the end you will face
live for today, don't worry my friend
for life is a story for which there's no end

AMONG MY BOX OF MEMORIES

Among my box of memories
sits a book of unfilled dreams
things I planned so long ago
yet yesterday, it seems

Though this book lay dusty
and the bindings come unwound
each pen mark says that of long ago
a treasure that I found

Dreams that meant so dear to me
each a goal to reach in life
to grow up have a happy home
some children and a wife

To be the best at what I do
and what I do it shall define
to never judge my fellow man
because his beliefs are not as mine

Never turn away from a hurting friend
be there to help when he's feeling hurt
for one day it might be him you need
and from his back perhaps, his shirt

So always remember there's those up there
without a day of new dreams
I stop and realize as I read my goals
I've accomplished everything

WOULD YOU STILL LOVE ME

Would you still love me if I couldn't tie my shoes
if you had the chance to leave or stay
which one would you choose
and when my body's frail and weak
and I can no longer stand
would you turn away from me
or would you take my hand
would you talk to me each night
even though my words not clear
and each new sunlit day
would you still call me dear
would you still look at me
and smile just because
would you understand my ups and downs
and know I will never be as I once was
when time takes its toll on me
can I count on you being there
I know to ask so much of you
and so much to ask unfair
the toll it takes, the time unknown
but together we can make it through
but still a choice, I ask my dear
would you still love me if I couldn't tie my shoe

I LIVE WITHIN MY TEN BY TWELVE

I live within my ten by twelve
I call my comfort zone
my little room where I go to think
or when I want to be alone
my little sanctuary
my own place to be myself
pictures posted on my walls
old mementos on the shelf
reminding me of who I was
and things that were so dear
in my little ten by twelve
there's nothing for me to fear
occasionally I venture
to the outside world now and then
but the feeling of discomfort
brings me hastily back again
my friend is my computer
the keys, write what's on my mind
I tell my thoughts, my deepest fears
or stories of my prime
I don't have much but what I do
is quite enough for me
friends in groups who are always there
and my family
I like my walls I built within
each needs a place of solitude
where they can seek the refuge
of the swinging of their mood,
outside I feel I'm being judged
with every move I make
in my little ten by twelve
my smiles are never fake

DON'T PUT ME OUT TO PASTURE YET

Don't put me out to pasture yet
my life is far from done
the many ways I look at it
it's only just begun
I learned to crawl before I walked
and so shall I once more
learn to live the best I can
as I did before
though it may not be as perfect
as it use to be
I will learn to live my life
that is the best for me
I know I cannot change the past
or take away the pain
I can learn to live with it
for there is no one here to blame
only myself to bare the guilt
if I refuse to try
and waste the good time I have left
repeatedly asking why

ELEVEN RED ROSES

There's eleven dried roses
in her diary at home
one less a dozen
one stands alone
her love she has given
to a sailor at sea
who's off in the waters
home soon he will be
and in his duffel lies
a rose of bright red
wrapped in white paper
with the words that she said
forever I shall wait
for the return of my love
whether there it be on earth
or in heaven above
there shall be one less a dozen
till he shall return
for he holds the twelfth
with the love that yearn
many years pass
her diary, brittle and frail
many years more, no one knows
what is it might tell
then a fair maiden glimpse upon it
and opens it wide
and finds a dozen dried roses
with a note taped inside
my love has returned
by the luck of one single rose
whoever shall find this book,
I shall be wed in the garden where it grows

PARKINSON'S
IT WON'T DEFINE ME...

We shall always search for answers
though we may never find the facts
to why it is we have to live this life
where Parkinson's distracts

Some might deny they have it
yet deep inside they know
but only when the signs kick in
I and when it starts to show

I refuse to let it run my life
though it is now a part of me
it won't define the man I am
or whom I'm going to be

I must go on living life
and adjust to fit it in
yes it's now a part of me
more likely till the end

But never do I lose control
and forget I chose my way
we must be compatible
and remind ourselves each day

THE MERMAID'S TRAP

Her eyes they entrap you
of emerald green
yet hidden behind them
she's evil and mean
the look of an angel
they glisten and glow
she'll entrap you in her web
and pull you below
a beauty of nature
the sea is her home
a many of sailors fell
for her heart made of stone
she lures you in
with the promise of love
then brings you deep down
from the waters above
you follow her down
till the waters too deep
to her waiting castle
in her dungeon you let keep
and soon word is spread
of another sailor, lost at sea
i am a prisoner of love
the mermaid and me

THE BOOK OF ME

Each of us we're all the same
yet different in every way
if i was to write a book on life
only I know what it shall say
it is my story between the cover
each of us has our own
we only see the outer shell
the life of others lay unknown
a library of life it seems
a look into the soul
a book that tells of where I've been
and tells me where I'll go
if you were to choose a book to read
in this library of many
would you choose your once again
in this library of plenty
each page tells of joyful times
from birth until this day
and of those who left us way to soon
and those for whom we pray
but in their place comes birth and growth
a new life to begin
one steps out that's what life's about
for each a new steps in
for each we have our bad times
but times there is more good
so would i want a different book
I wouldn't if I could
don't claim I'm always happy
in the pages you can see
I may glance another book
but I'll keep the one of me

BUILDING BACK A MOUNTAIN

Is it the fact that what were going through
keeps our mind at unrest
or perhaps the fact deep down inside
we know we'll have to be our best

Chances are we'll make it through
with the will and a helping hand
a lot of comfort from a friend
and those who understand

Some days you may feel thankful
yet there's those who will bring you down
its hard to keep your spirits up
with those such ones around

It might hurt to say there is no longer a need
remember it is you that you are trying to repair
and if they truly are a friend
the next time they'll be there

You're building back a mountain
a shovel might be slow
but if that's all you have to build
then that's the way to go

Many times you may miss a step
and try to tunnel through
but building back your mountain top
no short cut will do

WHERE A PERIOD WOULD DO

I'm more of a man then I use to be
for I've more burdens upon my back
and wake to face more unfulfilled dreams
yet keep my life on track

Each day I wake to another sunrise
as yesterday is spent
and tell myself it's a brand new day
so far it's a hundred percent

Don't put a question mark at the end of each day
when a period will do
turn the page from yesterdays
for today just start out new

MY LIFE IS LIKE A CIRCUS CLOWN

My life is like a circus clown
I could paint me a smile when I'm feeling down
and no one here could really see
the awful hurt inside of me

I could smile and laugh and tell a joke
though deep inside my heart is broke
I could put on a one man show
if tears run down they'll never know

to be the wiser to the fact
the smile of the clown is just an act
till the circus tent is done and gone
I'll wear my mask and carry on

And hope soon I can remove the paint
of this lonely smile that really ain't

IT'S THREE A.M. NO SLEEP AGAIN

The sun outside my window gives the time away
but not today it's three am
another wrestles night rolling round in bed
things go through my head, no sleep again

They give me pills to ease my pain
but don't help my brain, I'm up till dawn
I put a pot of coffee on to start my day
half gone away, I shuffle on

I spill half my coffee before I reach my chair
but I don't care, I've things to do
I drink my coffee as I watch the morning news
I get the blues, put on my shoes

I feel sorry for myself, sometimes I cry
I don't know why, it's not that bad
I wake up and I should feel that is a gift to me
I'm home and free, I should be glad

Then I think of those who never had the chance
to greet the morning sun, or love someone the way I do
now each time I'm down and pain comes around
I put myself in their shoes

The sun outside my window gives the time away
but not today, and that's ok

HOW FAR TO THE END OF HEAVEN

How far to the end of heaven
where might it begin
does it go on forever
or is it a circle with no end
is there a place out there that's somewhere
yet nowhere at all,
if you reach the end, is that the beginning
or perhaps there's just a wall
a place where old stars gather
for their time to shine is done
or do they join to form from millions of others
and combine into one
each set in a perfect place
and yet nothing to hold it there
and come the evening sunset
like clockwork you still see its glare
like life and its many wonders
who are we, why are we here, we ask
why are we so alike, yet so different
as well as our task
there must be a sun to keep us from
the darkness and the cold
there must be new stars born
to replace those of old
I believe each has his purpose
in this circle of life, not by chance you see
everyone has a special purpose
here for this world to be
nor do I believe we were meant to be alone
for new life, everything takes two
life was never meant to live it alone
together is how life grew

IT'S NOT FUNNY ANY MORE

We use to laugh and chuckle,
when we go places that we been
and forget what it was we came for
the minute we got in
or searched for our pair of glasses to find
they're on top our head
or get half way through a book
then find it's one that you read

But now it's not so funny
it's become a daily part of life
I no longer have a memory
that was sharp as a knife
so many times i stop and ask
what I came in here to find
no matter how hard I try I can't remember
am I losing my mind

I put things in my safe place
where I'm sure I won't forget
but that's been several weeks ago
I still ain't found them yet
why cant I forget the things
like the hurt that I've been through
yet I always tend to forget the names
of those I've always knew

I forget things I do daily
like take my medicine as I should
and if I make a list to remind me
I forget it, so that does no good
so if you never get a call my friend
to say they put me in my plot
it's not that I didn't care at all
it's just that I forgot

WHEN I WAS YOUNG

When I was young
love I didn't know
I kept no track of time
I had no place to go
chased kites through fields
to catch the wind
what I wouldn't give
to be that young again
I had my little dreams
but didn't see the doubt
I'd keep my childhood ways
but soon my youth ran out
and now I look back
to when all the youth was mine
and wish that I'd have known
that I'd run out of time
and now most the day
I sit here in my chair
and think it to myself
how life just isn't fair
although now I've lived
my better days
I'm still a child at heart
I find in many ways
I think of the love I had
all the places that I've been
my mind is full of empty fields
I still run against the wind
but now I'm much older
than I am young
I walk a memory of my past
what have I become

THE PREACHER MAN

The preacher man says that bad days are coming
in this world that were living in
I only have but one simple question
where the hell has he been

the rich man wants to take the poor man's money
the poor man's just trying to survive
he turns to stealing from his own brother
for the sake of keeping his family alive

We send our young to fight for our freedom
and bring them back in a body bag
if they are one of the few to make it home
they face streets filled with gangsters flags

The red white and blue stands for the honest man
ones who fought for our liberty
and those that thought here at home
they thought they fought to be free

But how many cities would you walk after dark
or cross a line where gangs claim is theirs
yet they don't really exist, though they're there
every day
and the killings going on there for years

If we want to be free why not start here at home
if the gangs want to fight they can
just keep our men who fight for America here,
believers of our freedom
send the gangs to fight in foreign lands

Keep the men and the money where it belongs
here at home
poverty would dwindle, so would crime
take those non American believers and offenders

send them to war to do their time

STATUE TO A HEADSTONE

It takes cold hard steel and a hammer
to chisel a statue from a piece of stone
so goes the life of the working man
who works his fingers to the bone

Most just want to earn a living,
an honest day's work for his pay
just wants paid for the hours he's given
for his honest eight hour day

The scars the scratches and the blood
are trophies of the price that he's paid
broken bones, days spent away from home
that's the path that a working man's made

They're those who would rather kill his brother
and steal instead of an honest way of life
there's still blood and bone, but it's not his own
instead of a statue, he makes a knife

And the one who only seeks an honest living
only becomes another victim of a crime
the steel and hammer chisels now a name into stone
while he who took the honest man is out in a short time

SOMEWHERE A FRIEND WEEPS

dedicated to those who suffer from depression

Somewhere a friend weeps
but no one hears his cries
it is wrong, he's so strong
he holds it all inside

All he'll say is he's ok
but deep down he's come undone
he's fought life's every battle
and every battle he's won

He's got his pride, he keeps inside
every hurt and pain
no need to help him, he'll get through
no need him to explain

Yet his eyes tell of sorrow
he says tomorrow he will be just fine
he'll seek a friend to help him mend
that friend was mine

Tomorrow came I thought the same
as they have the times before
but for him it never did
he won't suffer any more

Just someone to listen was all he was missing
to see through foolish pride
but he's a strong man
he can do it, just keep it inside

ANGELS AND BUTTERFLIES

Angels and butterflies
I know they're there, I don't ask why
I think about them when I cry
I love angels and butterflies
they always calm me when I'm down
each time I hurt they come around
they never even make a sound
if you look they can be found
every night ,before I sleep
after I ask my soul to keep
I listen but don't hear a peep
every night before I sleep
the beauty of their graceful flight
the butterfly a magical sight
the angels gleam you see at night
tells me every things alright
when I go I won't ask why
I won't hurt and I won't cry
I'll fly away and say good bye
with angels and butterflies

FOR THE FIRST TIME AGAIN

Perhaps I'm my own maker
through the choices that I've made
should I have chose a different path
in this roll I played

Every step I took
lead me closer to where I am
now I set my compass
will it lead me back again

The path I took in life
were not paved in solid gold
I chose to walk the paved one
now I shall be bold

No maps no printed directions
just a mind and will to be
the person that I'm looking for
the man inside of me

I seek to see the same things
go the same places I have been
but see it for the first time
as i see them once again

I stood beneath the mountains
as I looked at the beauty high above
now I wish to climb that peak
and touch that which I love

THOUGH YOUR TEMPLES MADE OF STONE

Though your temples made of stone
mine is made of skin and bone
given life and promised death
from the day of my first breath

I'll worship not a structured place
I pray not each day ,nor say my grace
nor spend my life that's given me
I live it to the best of my ability

Why would a god put us here on earth
only to live it thanking for our birth
or worship him our whole life through
for something we've not seen nor knew

I do believe that there is such a place
that rules both us as well as space
we are far too perfect, by no mistake
could you imagine what that would take

A church is there to comfort souls
and worship that of which they chose
if they feel comfort ,where they kneel and pray
there is no wrong, each has their way

My house of worship is my mind given me
for I choose who I want to be
and if I falter, it's by fault of my own
for I am to blame, and me alone

Each their own temple of body and bone
each has the choice who rules the throne
and if there is a god above to take our souls
only those who have gone shall ever know

COME SIT AT MY TABLE FOR TWO

Shall you ever be down and find
you need someone to help you through
there is always room for all friends
at my table for two

You are always welcome
there's plenty to share
the servings are kindness and love
and people who care

Come sit at my table
you shall always have a place
for the settings before you
are set with guidance and grace

YOU ARE THE DIAMOND

For you are a priceless diamond
in a simple world of stone
jewels of many colors
yet one clear one stands alone

To find a setting worthy
to entrust upon its hold
can only be of platinum
and etched with solid gold

The precious stone of beauty
with its cuts yet not a flaw
once a simple piece of coal
now the strongest of them all

The clearness its value
for there's nothing there to hide
just an image of life's work
no flaws left deep inside

Our life is such as this jewel at hand
they can't be found that way
Yet polish the scratches one by one
you shall become a diamond someday

ANGELS NEVER LIE

It's a rainy Sunday morning
as the church choir starts to sing
take me back to heaven
on a pair of angel wings

As they walk him past the alter
for his final journey home
six bells ring a dozen times
with a somber echoed tone

Each pew stands as
they slowly walk him down the aisle
the widow stands to send him off
as her tears fall in denial

As she reaches in her pocket
a note falls to the floor
in his note shall I pass before you
I'll wait for you at heaven's door

She looks up as she smiles
and says her last good bye
she knows he'll be there waiting
for angels never lie

SHE WAITS BEYOND THE FOREST EDGE

Just beyond the forest edge
beneath the tree line dark as coal
waits my princess, dressed in white
in the darkness, her gown shall glow

For two sunrises and one weary night
I travel the darkest trail
to reach the love of my beautiful mate
for soldiers are on my trail

I can hear the waters in the meadow
the clearing must be near
behind me the sound of a hundred hoofs
with their swords, I've just a spear

From the castle she has fled for me
relinquished her mighty crown
and rid herself of her cloak and cape of gold
in place, a tarnished white gown

For I see the glow of the moon through the trees
I've only but yards to go
the thundering hoof s fade in the distance
as I emerge to her beautiful glow

For now we are together forever
she wears no gold upon her head
no castle no crowns no fancy jewels
she rules upon our throne instead

GUMDROPS AND LOLLIPOPS

When I was just a lad
I'd cry like children do
my father would set me on his lap
and tell a story or two
the tears in my eyes
would soon change to a gleam
he'd put me to bed, tuck me in
and that story I'd dream

He would assure me that nothing
would come take me away
and until I was fast asleep
at the foot of my bed he would stay
and he promised me things
that made me feel he would always be here
I just call out his name
I would turn and he's there

I thought pain was so easy
to heal when I was a kid
I recall every day
all the things that he did
it was gum drops and lollipops
to heal all my pain
but even gum drops and lollipops
fall apart in the rain

And they don't heal the hurt
like they did as a lad
but they help me remember
all the love of my dad
each time I think of him
it takes me back again
to when I was just a lad
and I would turn and call to him

Just like gum drops and lollypops
they fade in the rain
but the memories of the good days
shall always remain
and some day I will see him
in the heavens above
and give him gum drops and lollipops
to show him my love

THE STRENGTH IS WITHIN YOU

You call a friend, for strength within
and hope this day will pass
but all along what keeps you strong
you see in the mirrored glass

The strength you hide lays deep inside
waiting for its release
its healing strong, was there all along
to administer, inner peace

Look no further than yourself
before you seek what is in your soul
the healings at hand, is in your command
so let it loose and let it show

Look in the mirror at the reflection you see
the first step to hope is there
the one that you see is who it should be
the person you see in the mirror

GOOD MORNING LIST

I woke up this morning
and I worked on down my list
I say good morning to all my friends
I know there's some I missed

But each ones just as important
for they are my heart and soul
I count on them throughout the day
more then they will ever know

I count on them for smile
when I'm hurt and feeling down
I count on them to talk to me
when no one else Is to be found

Perhaps I ask their help to often
and do they really care
I don't ask those questions
they are always there

There's no hesitation
should they need a shoulder or a hand
or perhaps a poem to pick you up
one you can understand

Each morning I find upon my list
another best friend I never met
although we've yet to meet in person
sometimes that part we forget

I am blessed to have such friends
from one cost to across the sea
their the biggest medication I have found
they are the strength in me

WHO PUT THE LEAD IN MY SHOES

I am use to going just about
anywhere I choose
but now I ask myself at times
who put the lead in my shoes

My feet they have a shuffle
that slows me to a crawl
I can't keep moving forward
it just drives me up the wall

But on a good day I can walk a mile
sometimes back again
but I set out on that stroll
I don't know how it comes or when

I wish I knew where it goes
all the strength I lose
so I've only have one question
who put the lead in my shoes

ARMED WITH JUST A PAD AND PEN

Armed with just a pad and pen
and a mind full of hollow pain
so many words, so many questions
yet still so many remain

Just beyond our breaking point
yet were rescued once again
the hurt, the relentless gnawing at our hope
yet were determined we will win

Each time the tides against me
no matter how hard I swim, it pushes me back to shore
but eventfully the tide shall go down again
then I shall chance the swim once more

It remains to me an answer
things aren't impossible to achieve if you try
don't swim out if the tide is high

Like the pad and pen, and the mighty sword
there's always two sides to everything
the hurt, the pain, the sorrow in life
or the happiness that life can bring

I compose of that which my mind only feels
and put it down so I may read what lays inside
when I am thankful, I write of joy given me
in times of grief, of the times I've cried

TOMORROW IS BUT A GIFT

The world will just keep spinning
it shall go around for eternity
its foolish to think that just for a blink
it would stop long enough for me

If I get off it shall just keep on going
my point will just pass me by
but if I wait long enough I know
I can get back on if I want to try

For every things a circle in life
what goes around comes again
so if you need time to clear your mind
jump back on once your setbacks mend

Don't miss the point of living
and don't get lost in the past
no matter how weak or strong you are
live for today, it's a wonderful task

The past will never be changed
tomorrow is still yet to come
today is the present, that's why it's a gift
and not given to everyone

SELF-SUFFICIENT MAN

I'm a self-sufficient man I could run a microwave
I buy two for one think of all the money I will save
I could invite my friends over have a perfect seven
course meal
a six pack and a pizza, on a two for one type deal
if I cut out the delivery fee, I can still make it before the
game
I'll pick it up, and bring it home, I'm sure they won't
complain
off I go too they'll be so proud, I make the perfect host
just a few blocks left to go, maybe three at the most
it should be just around this bend, that's where it was
before
maybe just a little further, couldn't be much more
damn time is running short, where the hells my map
she'll never let me hear the end, I'm sure to catch her
crap
you should of asked directions, I'm sure that's what
she's gonna say
it makes it so much easier, if you don't know the way
I'm a self-sufficient man dammit, I don't need someone
to tell me where I've been
shit , I've passed that place three times ,and here I go
again
ah finally made it home the game is over all my friends
are gone
and there awaiting me in all her glory, what took you so
long
and as I tell her all about my trip, I pop a beer and pass
her a can
I explain how the car broke down but I fixed it, I'm a self-
sufficient man

DEPRESSION THE GAME OF LIFE

Life's the only game I know
where you have the choice to win or lose
you're given many challenges in life
you could quit or go on if you choose

If you should decide not to take the chance
and refuse to even try
just remember this my friend
this game the stakes are high

The loser remains inside his shell
the winner moves ahead
the loser only sinks further down
with a heart full of loneliness instead

If you could read the play book,
and there's no opposing team
if it betters your chance to win
isn't that a player's dream

If you're not satisfied where you stand in life
join the game invite a friend
if it is the help you need to move on
instead of staying where you've already been

It's hard to play this game alone
the course at times gets rough
so if you ask someone to help
it's no shame when times are tough

And that's the game the choice is yours
do I win or lose or perhaps I just give in
I choose to keep on playing the game of life
I won't win if don't play, I'm in it till the end

HAPPY JUST BECAUSE YOU ARE

You ever thought of being happy
just because of who you are
and proud of what you have accomplished
and that you've come this far
you're not the one you use to be
your will to fight is strong
don't look back keep moving forward
it's time to move along
there's many goals ahead to reach
each a promise to fulfill
find it in your inner strength
to climb life's chosen hill
life still lays ahead of you
although the branches bend
they will never break and fall
no matter storm nor wind

IF SHE COULD ONLY SEE

There's a lady I know who makes ribbons and bows for
a living
all the mistakes that she happens to make, she is given

She takes them all home, and when she's alone she
makes beautiful things
like teddy bear ties, and silk butterflies, and beautiful
angel's with wings

When she gets them done, she's off on a run, to take
them to children each day
she won't charge a dime for her money or time, she
proudly gives them away

She sits for awhile as they give her a smile, and she
listen to their harmony
they tell her wonderful things for the gifts that she
brings, oh if only she could see...

PAPERS, PAGES AND PAMPHLETS

There's papers and pages, and pamphlets to tell how I
feel
explain to the doctor your ailments, he gives you a pill
you take it in stride because that's what you're
supposed to do
but how you feel deep down inside, they haven't a clue
the shaking you get, they say it gets better on meds
and the pain in your legs, they say it's all in your head
too tired to stay up, but to sore to try and get rest
you search through your friends names to find one who
knows best
but its three in the morning you find there's no one to
call
the ones that are still up are still up with no answer at all
its six o'clock now and through the window the morning
sun shines
I've got to eat breakfast, take meds, keep the queasiness
from my mind

I lay on the couch and finally my eyes start to take rest
from last night
I waste half the day getting ready, motivation doesn't
come till moon light
then once again I start the same routine over again
search through the names in the group to call on a
friend
there's paper and pages ,and pamphlets to tell how I feel

TEARS TO YOU

For all the times I felt like giving in
I felt I was through
you would come around and pick me up
here's tears to you

Most see hurt, they are too afraid
of falling in
they walk on by and ignore your cry
like it's a sin

In time of need their hearts could bleed
they're the first to cry
you see a tear roll down, they fear to wipe
it from their eye

A simple word not often enough heard
can ease the pain
there's nothing lost ,there is no cost
just all to gain

Just make it known they're not alone
and listen well
the faith they lack you could build it back
the time will tell

Be always there with time to spare if
someone's blue
a helping heart is the best place to start
here's tears to you

TWINS

Dedicated to my dear friend Patricia Williams

If you're to ask it all depends
is there a special bond between twins
do they really love and care
if one hurts do both twins share
I really have to say this to be true
for I've seen it in a pair that ii once knew
for both have hearts of gold
each courage's strong and bold
not a difference in one that I could see
in their hearts a special place to be
for god had made the first so well
he copied her so close you couldn't tell
now if you fall in love how do you choose
with their beauty and their heart you never lose
which one you love the most ,couldn't tell so love them
both
can you imagine them so young as a child
the tricks they could play to drive you wild
one runs out the back in blue
seconds later in the front she flew
so yes no doubt the bond is really there
it's a love that only special twins can share
a bond that's never broken
and special words that's never spoken
so remember every word that you say
cause if you're wrong , it's two you got to pay

AS THE WRITING'S ON THE WALL

After I had my doughnuts
I took a stroll all through the place
I don't see writing anywhere
perhaps they got erased

Says there's some writing
in between the lines
I'm looking straight at it
I don't see it, I'm going blind

I don't know why she up and left
I let her do everything for me
let her cook and clean my mess
she's gonna miss me wait and see

Don't I listen when you tell me you still care
and let you always give me a big kiss
and let you scrub my back till I'm done
and tell you all the spots you missed

You never been gone this long before
it's been the longest day of my life
when you coming back, all the dishes in a stack
ok, its hard to live without a wife

LOVED ME ALL ALONG

I think I will make it now
the clouds have all gone away
and now with you by my side
things will be ok
I shouldn't have ran from you
when you gave me your hand
but I didn't know
deep down you would understand

You always were there
you loved me all along
to doubt you this way
now I know I was wrong
you're love for me
was always there
I should have known
you would always care

Come hold my hand
come walk along my side
and never let go of me
I'll wipe the tears we cried
we can hold on to each other
till morning light
with you next to me
my worries are lost in the night

The love I thought we lost
and was forever gone
I know now deep down
was still there all along
you gave me the strength
to make it through anything
we can challenge the world
and what the day might bring

Together there's not much
that we can't do it seems
just close our eyes
and fill our unfinished dreams
I'll stand by your side
as the nights grow colder
I'll always be here
so rest your head on my shoulder

I will keep on loving you
even when our days are through
I know I was wrong
you loved me all along

THIS DAY IS FOR ME

I wake in the morning and put on my clothes
the same way I've done all my years
a little bit slower a little more pain
sometimes it brings me to tears

But I get out of bed as I wipe them a way
I haven't a place for my sorrow
I shuffle to the kitchen, for my first cup of tea
the anger will wait till tomorrow

But today I won't let disappointment fill in
and define how my days going to be
I'm going to start living how I want to live
by god, this day is for me

IS MY REFLECTION MY SOUL

Gaze upon the water's edge,
I can't help but notice my own reflection
staring back at me,
for each smile, every move, it looks upon me
for I cannot break it,
I reach to it in the exact moment it reaches back
I touch its softness upon the ripples it replies the same
it makes me stop, to ask myself, am I staring at my soul
for I can toss upon it rocks and stones yet once the
ripples have cleared
it takes back the shape of me again, it hasn't felt a thing
isn't that what a soul is for, but why do I feel all the pain
is my reflection a soul reminder of what I will be again
I look at it and cant believe how perfect it appears
but then I stop to realize
I am staring down at me

NOT MUCH INTO YOUR LIFESTYLE

Wouldn't trade my cowboy boots
for your business suit and tie
even though times are tough
I'm tough and getting by

And your Cadillac won't pull my trailer
or haul my bales of hay
I got better ways to spend
my hard earned money any way

You brag about your cigar
cost a fifty dollar bill
and you light it with a twenty
just to give yourself a thrill

Well back home we call that crazy
we have our country pride
the only time we show off
is on a horse that ain't been tried

We pay our dues with work and sweat
busting but all day
we don't want your charity
we like to earn our pay

and we still drink our beer from a pop top can
don't need no crystal glass
and if you can't shake my neighbors hand
then you can kiss my ass

TAKE TIME FROM THE CITY

The bus driver comes on and tells us were here for the
evening
the weather outside is to rough to go on our way
doesn't have the exact time that we will be leaving
I find myself a small corner, for our short stay

With my head phones on I listen to all of my memories
it brings me back to the times when I was a lad
but now in my prime most of my music is theories
those of the songs I would adhere to as memories of
dad

I take a glance at the children at play at the station
and the parents punching numbers to make use of their
time
they sit on the bench, complaining about wasting time
for vacation
as if they had done some sort of crime

Never slow down, all the people who live in the city
they rush around with often no place to be
the young lads in tailored suits, the girls all try to look
pretty
to many things to do, the beauty, there's no time to see

I'm just a country man, I don't take for granted these
things
every things beautiful if you take time to look you will
find
sitting here waiting, I see the beauty of all that it brings
I pull off my head phones and shuffle myself out to the
line

I hear the bus driver call to us to say we are soon on our

way
as the men in their suits all rush to the door
the lads and the ladies, scurry to go, with no words to
say
and we are off once again, but I have a different outlook
than before

Time isn't wasted, if even if that's all you have left to
give
there's plenty of time to enjoy what might come your
way
after all isn't that the reason were put here to live
so stop if you want to live every minute of every day
WE'RE ALL THE SAME YET DIFFERENT IN EVERY WAY

Each of us ,were all the same, yet different in every way
if I was to write a book on life only I know what it shall
say
it is my story between the cover, each of us has our own
we only see the outer shell, the life of others lay
unknown
a library of life it seems a look into the soul
a book that tells of where I've been, and tells me where
I'll go
if you were to choose a book to read in this library of
many
would you choose yours once again in this library of
plenty
each page tells of joyful times, from birth until this day
and of those who left us way to soon ,and those for
whom we pray
but in their place comes birth and growth a new life to
begin
one steps out that's what life's about for each a new
steps in
for each we have our bad times, but times there is more

good

so would I want a different book, I wouldn't if I could
don't claim I'm always happy in the pages you can see
I may glance another book, but I'll keep the one of me

HOMELESS HERO

It's not a shock, there's those who mock
the homeless and the poor
they haven't a clue, what he use to do
or the times he spent at war

They stand around and put him down
they treat him that of a lesser man
no shoes no coat no shave
he lives the best he can

As tears flow from his cheek
he would tell of the life's he saved
he's nor coward nor weak
why he fought to keep us free

Yet now he sleeps the empty streets
asking for money on his knees
he offered his life to keep us safe, yes we're doing fine
reason be that we are free

Are those unknown crowded at the soup line
so don't judge a man you don't understand
there's a story in every soul
that one you mock, that sleeps on your block

LIFE IS LIKE A CASTLE

Life is like a castle
there's few that we let in
stone and steel to keep us safe
few are welcome back again
inside the comforts of my fortress
I am safe and sound
only when I feel the trust
does the draw bridge come down

Uutside these walls life goes on
with no clue what lay inside
my gates are always closed
to keep in my foolish pride
now he walls that held so strong
are slowly crumbling down
the strength of my foundations weak
its cracking all around

I must leave my castle and seek
the shelter that lays out side these walls
before my castle comes crumbling down
and my whole life just falls
I've hidden in the darkness far too long
for outside they welcome me
they help to build my castle once again
the way it ought to be

You're the king of your own castle
but does no good if you're alone
your heart and mind is that kingdom
not the brick, steel, or stone
if you feel the comfort lies inside the walls
leave the draw bridge down
at least you will find the help you need
should the wall come tumbling to the ground

MANY THOUGHTS A SIN

As the sun wakes to peer across the
glistening of your skin
I awake with many thoughts
perhaps many thoughts a sin

As I glance upon your eyes
many desires fill my mind
for your beauty like an angel
such a treasure hard to find

To touch upon your lips
to start the morning with a kiss
yet another just because
for a day I might have missed

You wrap your arms around me
your hold is met with mine
together our we feel comfort
as our bodies enter twine

The comfort of your touch takes me
places I only dreamed until now
fantasies and fairy tales, never true
until this day somehow

In my mind I've made love to you
at least a thousand times, it seems
yet each one like the first one
if perhaps only in my dreams

But dreams they could be magical
a start to that which is left for us to feel
and the dreams for which I had
are now becoming real

MONDAY MORNING GLOOM

It's that Monday morning moon
that leads to the mid day feeling of gloom
I have my cup of liquid life
the aches stab me like a knife

The pills I took hours ago
seems today their working slow
it throws me off once again
breakfast at eight yet now its ten

I finally feel the meds affect
but now I'm sleepy my life's a wreck
and as I try to understand
I wake to take my meds as planned

It's hard to grasp the days half gone
and I still have nothing on
as I shuffle to grab a bite to eat
get dressed and fight to put shoes on my feet

The day has went so quickly by
nothing accomplished no matter how hard I try
but then I guess I have no right to complain
some live a storm, I've only had rain

So when the sun brings the brand new day
I should be thankful, kneel and pray
that each day I have the chance to once more
to do things I never had the chance to before

FOLLOW ME IF YOU DARE

Follow me if you dare
for I see things that isn't there
there is no trickery of the mind
let me take you back in time

Where I will show you a simple fact
how in time you can look back
each time you gaze upon a star
it looks close to the touch but oh so far

Unimaginable miles yet we see its light
from a far off distance in the darkest night
how can it be its so far out in space
every night it's found in the exact place

Now here's the part I want to share
do you realize what you see is no longer there
what you see is long since gone
yet it appears each night with its light so strong

You are looking back in time
before the star burnt out and lost its shine
it just takes a simple mind
and exciting things I'm sure you'll find

Just look no further than yourself to realize anything is
possible if you believe it to be

IN GOD'S GARDEN

In God's garden wild flowers grow
there's those of every kind
the colors stretch for miles around
such beauty you may never find

A canvas on the painted hills
the brush of gods own hand
each one as bright as the next
beauty scattered throughout the land

The winter coats the marvels
yet in spring time every year
the blooms come back once again
that spreads so far and near,

A circle of nature best
the brush upon gods hand
reminds us of his miracles
without the touch of man

The flowers dry the seeds shall fall
only to be blown across the way
the rain shall fall, the sun shall shine
and soon it to will bloom in May

Without the hand of man it grows
nature is its best keeper of this land
no need to change it to fit our needs
when Mother Nature is in command

WORKING MAN'S SHIRT

I was raised with my hands
in mud and dirt
born to wear
a working man's shirt

Scares and scratches
the hurt and pain
was never an option
just part of life's game

The hurt, you worked through it
no time to cry
there's things to get done
just wipe your eyes

You work till your feet
are blistered and sore
and still keep going
till you can't anymore

WHEN IT'S TIME TO MEET MY MAKER

When it's time to meet my maker
and the man upstairs calls
I'll be my undertaker
so throw in my boots and overalls
don't want to keep him waiting
I'll be waiting with my shovel in hand
I'm going to be his own grounds keeper
I'm going to till the promise land
going to plant them rows of daises
we been pushing up all this time
going to keep them grapes a growing
going to make that sacred wine
and the wheat fields are going to reach so tall
I going to make a lot of bread
instead of breaking off a little piece
we'll give them all a whole loaf instead
and if they have vacation time
I'll spend it on the farm back home
in my coveralls and shovel, making sure
every seed in the field gets sewn

WIPE THE DUST OFF MY DANCING SHOES

Gonna wipe the dust off of my dancing shoes
go down to the dancing hall
maybe I can't go disco anymore
but I can shuffle with the best of them all

And if I happen to slip now and then
I just say it's part of the groove
no one would be the wiser to know
that it wasn't part of the move

Soon everybody will be shuffling around
to a dance that fits my feet
word will spread for miles away
this dude's got a brand new beat

I think I'll wipe the dust off my shoes
my days aren't over yet
you can't give up unless you give it a try
and if you try, there's no regret

UNTIL YOU PROVE ME WRONG

I am friends with everyone
until they prove me wrong
if that's so i guarantee
we won't be friends to long
the first times always shame on you
the second shame on me
only a fool would hang around
to wait for number three

I never judge those i don't know
I've never worn their shoes
they have the right to be themselves
and lead the life they chose

I'll never lie if you ask me
but if you don't ask I won't tell
i leave the fire to kindle,
to keep the peace as well

to disagree to prove a point
to often turns just to win
many times there is no winner
just the loss of two good friends

so if you want to see who's right
and play that game with me
go ahead and raise your crown
you win, I shall decree

IN THE MIRROR

A thought crosses my mind
yet once again
as I rush to grab
my pad and pen,
I write each word
as is comes to me
as I stare in the mirror
at what I see
I'm doing well
for the life I lead
I'm far from rich
but I have what I need
and my aches and pains
there are a few
but each sunrise
my day is new
there's others who
this gift won't come
I am blessed to be
a lucky one
another day to kiss
those that I love
and pray to those
who are up above
I can smell the flowers
and taste the wine
hug the family
and the friends of mine
they say love now
for tomorrow might be too late
to show ones you love
why should you wait
or you will be too busy to notice when they're not here
when there's no reflection
in the mirror

HERE IN OUR TINY LITTLE TOWN

Today's another peaceful day
in our tiny little town
the shops set their tables out
as the coffee crowd comes around

People smiling, children playing
laughter everywhere
the early morning sun comes up
another day of love to share

But today there stands a different noise
a silent somber tone
as papers spread the word gets round
that chills us to the bone

Across the oceans waters
yet another senseless act
of only innocence were killed
in another foolish attack

Terrorist who take their lives
along with many more
yet never knowing what it was
they were dying for

Those that fell in their innocence
are prayed for the world round
each night I pray and thank god
there's peace here in our tiny little town

PLACES I'VE ALREADY BEEN

I sit at the front of the train to see the places we're going
while those at the back only see the places I've already
been
the sway of the trees outside, as the cold wind is
blowing
as I sit in the warmth, I recall memories of some of my
friends

Many hours pass as we finally arrive at the end of our
travels
the six o'clock train pulls in at quarter till nine
all of the business means tempers now start to unravel
as I reach for my suitcase, I hadn't noticed the time

Three extra hours of traveling just seeing all of life's
beauty
there's no extra charge as the conductor announces
were finally here
the city folk holler and yell though he's only doing his
duty
as I sit at the bar, I pop open a can of good cheer

Grateful my travels had showed me so many new
pleasures
and three hours free don't even cost me a dime
to travel along and see all of life's treasures
as I sat at the front and watched as we passed through
time

I sat at the front, so I can see where in life I was going
they sit at the back only seeing where I've already been

SHE COULD TEASE YOU OR PLEASE YOU

She could tease you or please you
in the wink of an eye
with her sultriest beauty
as she passes you by

A smile that would capture
most any mans desire
the glow of her eyes
like flames of a fire

Her lips glisten
so moist and yet firm
as they entrance you
there's nowhere to turn

To touch hers a gift
that few have received
only but a few
for she's never deceived

Such a angel as her
can only be earned
no second chance
she's never been burned

MY LIFE FEELS LIKE A PUPPET

My life feels like a puppet
hanging by sticks and strings
controlled by the puppet master
he can make me dance and sing

My hands they move by just a tug
my walk is like that of a child
for I've no control of where I go
my hands and feet go wild

My knees they bend ,sometimes at will
or at times they wobble and shake
as if my puppet master wants to see
just how much of this I'll take

When the strings are tight and sticks are straight
I get around just fine
but when they tangle and sticks are bent
I it changes this world of mine

I shall cut the strings that hold me
and control my everything I do
and learn again to live my life
my days are far from through

Now I am the puppet master
the sticks and strings I hold
from here what I do in life
I myself control

A HURT DEEPER THAN PAIN

There's a hurt that grows deeper than pain
with a few words I'll try to explain
when the things that you do are things I use to
it constantly gnaws at my brain

If you tell me I can't then I'll try
with no rhyme or reason why
I'll go along just to prove I'm still strong
even if it hurts till I cry

Don't tell me I won't then I will
regardless of how I might feel
I'll prove that I can, just to prove I'm a man
without making it a big deal

How far can I go till I'm done
I'll keep going till I fell I've won
perhaps even more just to make sure
and say it was all done in fun

The harder you push I will pull
my glass is not half empty it's full
and till it is gone, I'll keep moving along
then when you say I gave up that is bull

If I happen to throw a small fit
it's only because I never quit
I might stop and rest but I try my best
slower perhaps just a bit

But I'm still running this race
so what if I don't get first place
as long at the end, I'm standing, my friend
I finish with love and grace

LISTEN TO THE RAIN

As the morning hours pass swiftly by
I find my chores half done
and soon I find the day is gone
as I await the setting sun

But clouds move slowly over head
there's a beauty that I can't explain
I grab my favorite book in hand
as I listen to the pouring rain

The sound of drops against the glass
comforts me as I read
and curled up upon my lap
my cat a friend, indeed

I glance the pages of my book
but my thoughts wander astray
the comfort of the gentle rain
takes my thoughts away

If only for the evening hours
I owe myself this peace of mind
to take my mind and wander
and leave all my sorrows behind

and tomorrow shall the sun appear
I'll work the whole day through
and perhaps the evening hours my friend
will bring peace once more to you

TAKE THE WORLD FOR A RIDE

Any road will take you where you're going
though it might not take you where you want to be
the road won't change its final destination
the change is up to me

I take a look at all the things around me
everything is set in its place
unless I choose to adjust them to fit my needs
I can't complain of the consequences I face

I have the choice to change that which I choose
they won't change for me
if I change the direction that I'm headed
I will end up where I want to be

Don't stand still and let the world pass you by
hop on and take it for the ride
and if by chance you move a little slower
at least you're keeping stride

SHE WAITS FOR HER LOVER

She patiently sits on the bench as she waits for her
lover
it's been several days and he's been far away
off to the city he's gone to visit his mother
he's due to arrive on the twelve o'clock train today
she doesn't know it but he's got a ring for her finger
to marry her would she if he asked to take her hand
the train station fills with those who rush or just linger
he wants to marry and take her to a far away land
the whistle blows as the train pulls into the station
her eyes all aglow as he steps into the door way
her livelihood was that of a wealthy family's maiden
would she be happy in a far away land or rather she stay
they hold tight the arms that many days lay so lonely
he turns to his lover and slowly get down on his knees
he slips on the ring as he asks her to be his one and
only
and in his soft voice, forever shall hold you please
the fair maidens answers with tears flowing down from
her chin
as they leave the station, another maiden sits and waits
for her lover

I AM BUT A HUMBLE PERSON

I am but one humble person
set in my own way
when I reach my final destination
you'll hear no trumpets play
no marching band, or big parades
to say a big goodbye
no sobbing crowds or church bells
no one there to cry
in my heart I did my best
I'm proud of what I've done
no less, no more, each challenge
he gave, I've won
I do not fear the day he calls
to take my soul away
for then I'll hear the angels sing
and his trumpets play

SHE'S MYSTICAL AND MAGICAL

She's mystic and magical
in her own way
an un tarnished beauty
till she comes out to play
her eyes black and evil
as the darkest of coal
whisper so soft
as she calls for your soul
lips that glisten
and dare for a kiss
the pleasure so sensual
yet leads to abyss
she leads you to darkness
her pleasure, she fills
entrapped by her beauty
enticing her thrills
she pulls you in
by your lust and desire
she sets you ablaze
then she kindles the fire
come the morning
in the light of the day
like a princess asleep
in her bed there she lay

TO MY DEAR FRIEND EMM PAUL

Through all the things that ail me now
I feel selfish to complain
I look back at all my good years
and those that still remain
I've seen what life can give me
I took it all in stride
but never has it crossed my mind
all the pain you hide
my pain I can grin and bear
or just simply walk away
but to live it each and every hour
and hope for just a day
you pray that perhaps a miracle
shall find its way to him
and give him back his memory
of where it was he's been
strength and pain of losing someone
yet he stands before your eyes
the days on end you ask yourself
does god hear my cries
for six long years he slept, was it here
or somewhere far away
if only for a little while
give him the memory to say
I shall never more complain
the hurt that I may go through
for I will never have the strength
of someone such as you

I LAUGH WHEN I SHAKE

I laugh when I shake
what else can you do
I shuffle when I walk
but each day I make it through
for its just a thing
I must fit in my day
but just because it's there
I still do things my way
people might stair
and sometimes may ask
isn't living with it
a hell of a task
if you let it, it is
but I never give in
I fought all my life
and this fight I'll win
maybe I can't do all the things
I once done in my youth
but I couldn't have regardless
to yell you the truth
it isn't picky
on whom it might choose
but if you fear it's too strong
it's a battle you'll lose
I have it
by no choice of my own
I do have the choice
of how to go on
I fit it in and make it
part of my plan
it don't run me
I'm too stubborn a man
some day maybe
I will slow to a crawl
but until that day happens
I won't put up a wall
I no longer worry

of what will be or might
I take each day given
and live it in spite
tomorrow's not here yet
and yesterday's gone
today is the gift a present
so keep going strong

PARKINSON'S, CAN YOU CATCH IT?

I strolled along the parkway walk, when
I came amongst a family on a warm summers day
the parents appearance, that of upper class
the child dressed to play
they stopped to glance upon the water's edge
where the geese had gathered for their feed
and turned to see me standing there
and kindly asked what do you need
I exclaimed it nothing to worry about
just a Parkinson's attack
as I told him more about my shaking spells
I noticed he took a few steps back
I won't catch it will I dad
if I do will it ,will it ever go away
will I be able to go outside
will I shake, can still go out and play
the father took him by the shirt
as he turned and started to say good bye
just then I heard the whimpering sound
of the child start to cry
the father hands him a cloth
to wipe the hand he shook
and turned once more and waved good bye
with a discouraging look
if the parents won't take the time
how will the children understand
when we reach out to shake your hand
it's only but a hand

TOO MUCH TIME ON MY HANDS

As I sit here with too much time on my hands
and too much on my mind
I wonder if I would have made different plans
what difference in life I would find

As I go through my list of things I would change
the thought then occurs to me
no matter how many things I rearrange
it wouldn't be me that you see

For I am who I am in this life that I was given
and that's not on my list
so maybe I should put it at the top and start living
the life that I have missed

I passed my own self right on by
dreaming of who I am not
I could dream but no matter how hard I try
you can't let yourself be forgot

Everyone has a future to live be it an hour or hundred
years
so plan it for you, and you alone
don't try and shed someone else's tears
you have enough of your own

NEVER WENT TO BED HUNGRY

TO MY FATHER, MAY HE REST IN PEACE
FRANKIE LEE BRYANT 1928 -1991

Never went to bed hungry
always had shoes upon my feet
maybe it wasn't the best there was
but it kept us off the street

My father worked all day long
to keep seven mouths well fed
never once heard him complain
he kept a roof over our head

He went off to fight three wars
then came back to face one of his own
by raising seven children
and try to keep a happy home

His hands were bruised and callused
but he worked until they bled
all day long he made an honest pay
he worked till he was red

So if you want to complain about your life
make sure you look at where others been
then tell me how rough it is
maybe you will think again

IS CLOSE TO HEAVEN

Brush the hair back from your shoulders
tell me what you're thinking now
let our minds grow a little bolder
let's make love just show me how
I've never been this close to heaven
seems I'm knocking at its door
will I ever be forgiving
and if so I'll do it once more
hold me like you really missed me
kiss me like it's our first time
come closer like it should be
let's make love like we've got time
and when the sun comes up tomorrow
will you still be in my arms
will you wake in regrets and sorrow
or whisper to me all your charms

THIS IS A TRUE STORYOF WHEN I WAS 6 YEARS OLD

Here is a story
I've not often told
to recall these days
makes my blood run cold
do you believe in miracles
I'd have to say
yes I do
you see them each day
as a young child
of perhaps maybe five
I think back and still wonder
how did I survive
in a pond with some friends
and a tube as our boat
I wasn't worried I couldn't swim
the tube kept us afloat
playing around
such as young kids will do
the tube flipped over in the middle
I knew I was threw
I sank like a rock
to the bottom of the ponds floor
and I stood there just watching
all my friends looking from shore
what gave me the strength
and the air to walk out
in my mind it was
a miracle no doubt
I wasn't afraid at that time
it was as if on dry land
there wasn't a panic
someone was holding my hand
no one thought
I would come up alive
for the time I was under
not many survive

this is but one time
I thank god for another chance
to grow to be me
and dance one more dance

THE WONDERS OF HEAVEN

As I stare into the vastness
of a moon lit night
there's a multitude of beauty
in each twinkling of a light
each has its own wonder
each answer left to find
only seen but vaguely
by the imagination of the mind
how far must you go
till you can see the end
and once you are there
does it start all over again
is there really places
that is comforting as here
if so how far away
or better yet how near
would we be just as we are
if the world was in a different place
or would we be just as ignorant
no matter where in space
just a grain of sand
on a never ending beach
how much we need to learn
yet no one there to teach
perhaps outside our world
was meant only to be seen,
but left untouched by human hands
and viewed but in our dream
so many questions left to ask
the answer might be clear
everything was created
with perfection of god's hand
but it didn't suit us
so it was changed by man
you think if we were somewhere else
we would change the things we could
and if so would it be for worse

or for our own good
we were givin nature
to support the human race
if you can find an untouched land
you'll find a perfect place

WOKE UP WONDERING WHO I REALLY AM

I woke up this morning wondering
who I really am
I go back and search my life
to when it all began
I'm the child my mother loved
and held me in her arms
I'm the one my father raised
and kept me from harm

I'm the one who took my books
and gained the ways to live
I'm the one to understand
why not to receive ,but give
I've learned each day the choices
and which were right or wrong,
and a man needs not wealth and fame
to be considered strong

I learned through life that mistakes are made
but I learned from them
I learned its only foolish
if you try the same mistake again
I've done my life's work and what I did
in my life I'm proud
inside my soul I'm happy with what I have
I don't need a roaring crowd

Each day I wake and think to myself
how lucky that I am still me
I don't need the big things, or to run a race through life,
I'm where I want to be
every day's not perfect
but I have been given every day
and the chance to live it how I chose
and to live it my own way

What I've done in days that past
are days I've already lived
now I shall live each new day in life
there's a limit what he will give
this minute is the first of your future
make it the last one of your past
start today looking forward to times ahead
they don't forever last

Stan Bryant was born in 1960 into a large family of seven in Colorado Springs, Colorado. As a child, he spent time rock climbing, camping and fishing with his father and brothers. Re-locating to Southern California and Arizona, he worked full-time beginning at age 14. At 17 he joined the Navy for a four-year stint, serving on destroyers and air craft carriers in the Middle East. To occupy his free time dabbled in writing poems and songs.

After the service, Stan started working in housing construction and also ran his own cabinet making business for 12 years. A Parkinson's disease diagnosis came at age 49, but he continued to work until age 52. Still young, he put down his hammer and saw and picked up a pen and pad to record his daily struggles with PD, sharing them with PD groups. His choice was to give up on life or change it. This book is the result of that change.

Made in USA - Kendallville, IN
51162_9781519585974
07.21.2022 1628